Cakewalks, Two-Steps and Trots

for Solo Piano

34 Popular Works from the Dance-Craze Era

Edited by

David A. Jasen

DOVER PUBLICATIONS, INC.
Mineola, New York

PUBLISHER'S NOTE

Since the originals reproduced here are faithful historical documents as well as sources of enjoyment, the titles and artwork have not been changed even where they reflect the broader humor of their era, in which the nation was far less sensitive to jibes about minority groups. It is our belief that a mature understanding of our past is more fruitful than a falsification of history.

Bibliographical Note

Cakewalks, Two-Steps and Trots for Solo Piano: 34 Popular Works from the Dance-Craze Era is a new collection of music, selected and with an introduction by David A. Jasen, first published by Dover Publications, Inc., in 1997. The original publishers and dates of publications of the music appear in the Contents and on the individual covers and title pages.

International Standard Book Number: 0-486-29708-X

Manufactured in the United States by Courier Corporation
29708X02
www.doverpublications.com

INTRODUCTION

The field of popular music has always catered to singers and dancers. The exception, at the turn of this century, was ragtime—that extremely syncopated piano music that grew up in America's saloons and whorehouses. It was a happy music—music to socialize by and drink by, music that helped to create a comfortable and exhilarating atmosphere.

Social dancing of that time consisted mainly of the waltz, the polka and a two-step danced to a melody in 6/8 time. But when publishers added the designation "characteristic march and two-step" to their sheet music, the public understood that phrase to mean a syncopated piece, usually in 2/4. This was a new direction for America's devoted amateur piano players—an alternative to piano ragtime that was easier to play without sacrificing the rhythmic energy and stylishness of ragtime itself.

THE CAKEWALK

The cakewalk was the first dance of the era to be accompanied by a syncopated melody. With its minimal syncopation (not nearly as rhythmically complicated as the rag), the cakewalk offered a simple, singable tune that dancing couples found delightfully easy to follow. This new dance reached the public as a highly stylized theater dance—high-step strutting, exaggerated backward postures, by-play with canes—introduced in the mid-nineties by way of the all-black Broadway musical productions produced by the partnership of Bert Williams and George W. Walker. The cakewalk quickly became fashionable with the upper crust of society and a fad for the rest of the population.

With his first publication, "Rastus on Parade" (1895), composer-publisher Kerry Mills started the rage for this dance music, in time establishing the cakewalk as Tin Pan Alley's first major dance form, breaking the dominance of the waltz. Mills's "Rastus" had the further distinction of establishing what soon became an harmonic cliché of the cakewalk: it began in a minor key (D minor), then moved to the relative major (F major). Later composers retained the same harmonic relationship, following up with a trio section cast in the subdominant key. F. T. McGrath's "A Breeze from Blackville" (1899), for example, begins in A minor, moves to C major, then follows up with a trio section in F major.

It was Mills's "At a Georgia Campmeeting" (1897), however, that became the standard against which all other cakewalks were measured. This was the highly singable and danceable number, first rejected by all major publishers of the day, that firmly set up the publishing house of F. A. Mills for the next twenty years! (Kerry's real first names were Frederick Allen.)

In 1899, Mills's hit "Whistling Rufus" successfully competed with McGrath's "A Breeze from Blackville," Bernard Franklin's "Blackville Society," Ben Harney's "The Cake Walk in the Sky," Arthur Pryor's "A Coon Band Contest" (reissued in 1918 as a "jazz fox-trot"), Jean Schwartz's "Dusky Dudes," George Rosey's "A Rag-Time Skedaddle" and Abe Holzmann's "Smokey Mokes"—all winners in that "glorious year of the cakewalk."

In 1900, J. Bodewalt Lampe published his own "Creole Belles" in his hometown of Buffalo, New York, but it wasn't until Whitney-Warner, in Detroit, purchased and promoted the song the following year that it became a million-seller. While Kerry Mills went on to compose several Tin Pan Alley songs—"Meet Me in St. Louis" and "Red Wing" are two of his standards—he occasionally harked back to his cakewalking roots: 1909 saw the appearance of "Kerry Mills [no apostrophe] Ragtime Dance."

Although cakewalks, like marches, were often arranged for piano solo, their sheet-music covers typically displayed other instruments—usually trombones and banjos—signaling their popularity with marching and circus bands as well as string bands made up of violin, banjo and string bass. The earliest hits were popularized by the world-famous John Philip Sousa, who was responsible for the dance's popularity in Europe. Sousa himself detested the form but clearly saw its commercial possibilities, ordering Arthur Pryor (then Sousa's solo trombonist, later conductor of his own concert band) to write, direct and record cakewalk arrangements for the Sousa band.

TWO-STEPS

Lightly syncopated like the cakewalk and easy to dance to, the two-step shared status with the perennially popular waltz as the most popular ballroom dances of this century's first decade. Publication of two-steps fell mainly in the 1900–1910 decade, continuing up until World War I when the dance was succeeded by "animal dances" (the Turkey Trot, Bunny Hug, Grizzly Bear and so on) and the one-step.

Some of the most successful two-steps include S. R. Henry's "The Colored Major" (1900), Duane Crabb's "Fluffy Ruffles" (1907), "All the Money" (1908) by Raymond Birch (pen name of ragtime composer Charles L. Johnson), and William H. Tyers' "Panama" (1911).

TROTS AND GLIDES

Of all the various animal dances, the easiest to do and the most lasting was the Fox Trot. This enduring fad, which kicked off in 1914–15, intrigued such ragtime masters as Eubie Blake, who contributed "The Chevy Chase" and "Fizz Water," and Luckeyth ("Lucky") Roberts, composer of "Palm Beach" and "Shy and Sly." Other hits of the same years include Jack Glogau's "The Carus Breeze," Will Marion Cook's "Cruel Papa!," Fred Irvin's "Doctor Brown," "Ballin' the Jack" by Chris Smith and James Reese Europe, Melville Morris' "The Kangaroo Hop" and George L. Cobb's "Rabbit's Foot."A bit earlier than the Fox Trot onslaught, Cecil Macklin's terrifically popular "Très Moutarde" (1911)—better known as "Too Much Mustard"—covered all bases by promoting itself as a "One or Two-Step or Tango," its sheet-music cover suitably adorned with a fashionable dinner for two, complete with tuxedo, gown, enormous *chapeau* and champagne.

ELEGANCE

THE CASTLES ARRIVE

While racial stereotypes characterized the early years of cover art in the present collection—generally for the years 1897–1901—the next decade brought a decided shift. Elegantly dressed society women occupy center stage for the two-steps "Fluffy Ruffles" and "All the Money." A saucy society-dinner theme announces "The Lobster Glide." For "Très Moutarde," we are probably among the "swells" at Delmonico's. Elsewhere we are treated to hints of a fox hunt, a night on the town, a day by the elegant seaside.

In our covers of 1914, a new theme vies for the attention and consumer dollar of the masses: the stylish grace of professional dance partners Hathaway and McShane ("Ballin' the Jack") . . . the frolics of a fun-loving team dancing the "new society dance" ("Carolina Fox Trot") . . . tuxedoed McCutcheon and begowned Maxwell ("Originators of the Fox Trot") dipping and turning ("Trouville Canter"). When did the dance pros enter the scene?

Born in the waning years of the 19th century, dance team Vernon and Irene Castle (Vernon Blythe and Irene Foote) were largely responsible for the national craze for ballroom dancing when they returned to the United States from Paris in 1912. Their appearance as a sleek, compelling and physically attractive professional team gave public dancing a dimension far removed from the old-fashioned, conventional and easy dances generally familiar to the public. The Castles brought grace and beauty to an art carefully outfitted with fascinating rhythmic complexities, an endless variety of pair movements and new dance forms imported from South America. In the New York City area, the Castles established their own school (Castle House) and popular dance casinos atop a midtown theater (Castles-in-the-Air) and on the Long Beach boardwalk (Castles-by-the-Sea).

It was this star quality that led the New York publishing house of Joseph W. Stern & Co. to engage the Castles to pose for the covers of a series of dance tunes written by the two leaders of the Castles' personal orchestra of black players— James Reese Europe and Ford T. Dabney—and named for the team: "The Castle Walk," "The Castle Perfect Trot" and so on. In our cover collection, Europe's "The Castle Doggy" (1915) typifies the trend so powerfully triggered by these legendary dancers.

•

Cakewalks and two-steps, trots and glides—these are the wonderful syncopated dance tunes that filled a very special time and place in American popular music. As they looked backward to their roots in ragtime, they paved the way toward the musical signposts of the new century: the rise of Tin Pan Alley, Broadway's response to "the war to end all wars" and the song and dance innovations and crazes of the Roaring Twenties: the Charleston, the Black Bottom, the Varsity Drag.

Enjoy this unique treasure!

David A. Jasen

CONTENTS

CAKEWALKS AND TWO-STEPS

TROTS AND GLIDES

The Latest and Greatest Success

OF THE YEAR.

Rastus —on Parade.

.. BY ..

KERRY MILLS.

Characteristic Two-Step March for Piano.

WITH A VERSE TO ONE OF ITS QUAINT LITTLE MELODIES
WHICH CAN BE SUNG IF SO DESIRED.

5

Published by

F. A. MILLS,

45 West 29th St., New York.

LONDON: CHAS. SHEARD & CO.

TORONTO, CANADA—Anglo Canadian Music Pub. Assoc. Lt'd.

RASTUS ON PARADE.

by Kerry Mills

2

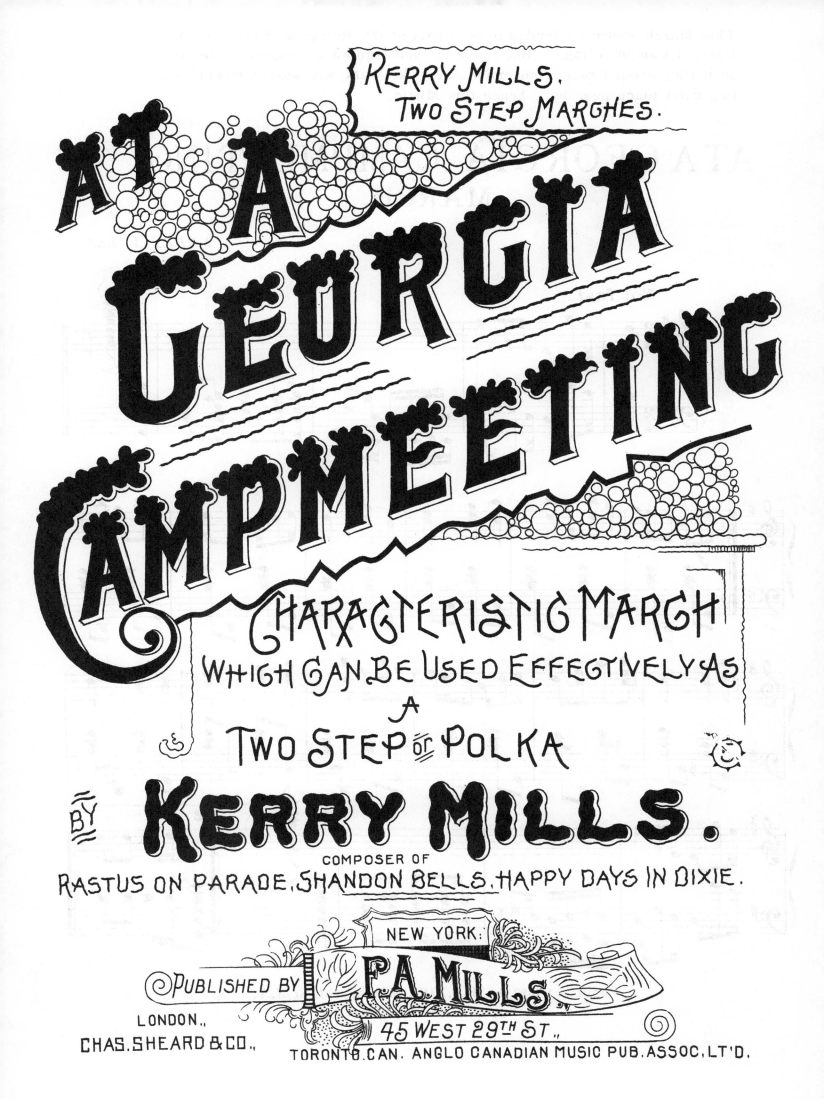

This March was not intended to be a part of the Religious Exercises "At a Georgia Campmeeting" but when the young folks got together they felt as if they needed some amusement. A Cake Walk was suggested, and held in a quiet place near by — hence this Music.

ATA GEORGIA CAMPMEETING
MARCH.

KERRY MILLS.

Not fast.

Copyright 1897 by F. A. Mills 45 West 29th St N.Y.
English Copyright secured.

Trio.

marcato.

BLACKVILLE SOCIETY

CAKE-WALK TWO-STEP

BY BERNARD FRANKLIN

BOSTON
G.W.SETCHELL
PUBLISHER

BLACKVILLE SOCIETY CAKE WALK

AND TWO STEP.

To be effective, must not
be played too fast.

INTROD:

BERNARD FRANKLIN.

A Breeze From Blackville

Cake Walk and Two Step

BY

F. T. McGrath.

PIANO SOLO .50

MANDOLIN SOLO	.25	BANJO SOLO	.35
TWO MANDOLINS	.35	" DUETT	.40
MANDOLIN & G.	.40	" & GUITAR	.40
TWO M'S AND G.	.50	TWO B'S AND G	.50

PUBLISHED BY

W. H. Teasdale Savannah, Ga.

STEWART & BAUER   C. S. MINTER   C. L. PARTEE MUSIC CO.   LOUIS F. WRIGHT
PHILADELPHIA, PA.   LITTLE ROCK, ARK.   KANSAS CITY, MO.   STATION A. WINSTED, CONN.
ROGERS & EASTMAN   BARROWS MUSIC CO.
CLEVELAND, OHIO.   Copyright 1899 by W.H. Teasdale.   SAGINAW, MICH.

Respectfully dedicated to my friend Mr. W. H. Teasdale, Savannah, Ga

A BREEZE FROM BLACKVILLE.

CAKE WALK AND TWO STEP

Arr. by W. H. Holmes.

F. T. McGrath.

Copyright **1899** by **W. H. Teasdale**.

14

TR1O.

MARCH A LA RAGTIME.

THE CAKE-WALK IN THE SKY.

A
RAG-TIME
NIGHTMARE.

WORDS
& MUSIC BY

BEN. HARNEY AUTHOR OF
"MR. JOHNSON TURN ME LOOSE" ETC.

PUBLISHED BY
M. WITMARK & SONS.

5

THE CAKE WALK IN THE SKY.

ETHIOPIAN TWO-STEP.

By BEN HARNEY.

Arr. by F. W. MEACHAM.

Tempo di Marcia.

A COON BAND CONTEST.

JAZZ FOX TROT

ARTHUR PRYOR.

Published 1918 by Emil Ascher, 1155 Broadway, N.Y.
Copyright 1899 by Arthur Pryor

TRIO.

Trombone Solo.

ARTHUR GOOTBROD

RESPECTFULLY DEDICATED TO **KERRY MILLS**, - THE MOST POPULAR MARCH WRITER OF THE DAY.

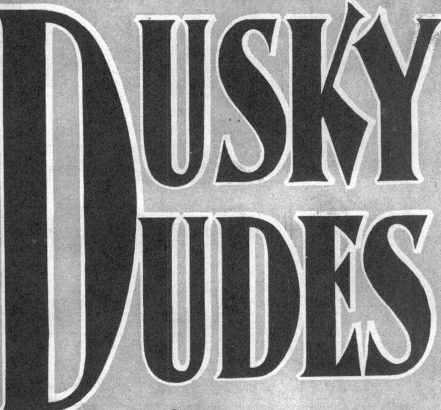

DUSKY DUDES

CHARACTERISTIC
CAKE·WALK
MARCH
AND
TWO·STEP
BY

JEAN SCHWARTZ.

PUBLISHED FOR
BAND, ORCHESTRA,
AND ALL OTHER
INSTRUMENTS.

INSTRUMENTAL.

VOCAL.

PUBLISHED BY

SHAPIRO, BERNSTEIN & VON TILZER

49 & 51 WEST 28TH STREET
NEW YORK.

A.H. GOETTING.   NATIONAL MUSIC CO   WHALEY ROYCE & CO   J. SINCLAIR.
SPRINGFIELD. MASS.   CHICAGO. ILL.   TORONTO. CAN.   MANCHESTER. ENG.

5

DUSKY DUDES.
CAKE - WALK.

by JEAN SCHWARTZ.

PIANO.

Trio.

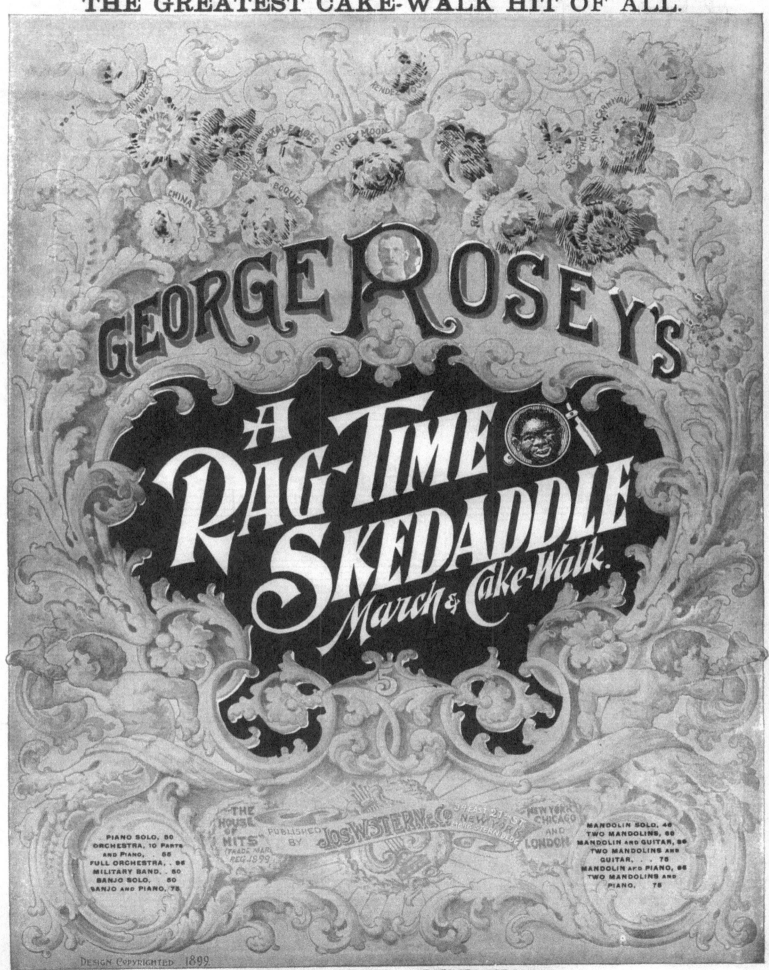

A Rag-time Skedaddle.

March and Cake-Walk.

by GEORGE ROSEY.

SMOKY MOKES

DEDICATED TO OUR MUTUAL FRIEND. ~ MR MONROE H. ROSENFELD.

PUBLISHED ALSO AS A SONG WITH HUMOROUS DARKY TEXT

PLAYED AT ALL THEATRES AND BY LEADING BANDS AND ORCHESTRAS.

PUBLISHED ALSO FOR ALL INSTRUMENTS INCLUDING MANDOLIN, GUITAR, ZITHER, BANJO, ORCHESTRA, BAND, ETC, ETC.

5

PHOTO BY HALL. N.Y. COPYRIGHT 1899 BY FEIST & FRANKENTHALER.

CAKEWALK AND TWO STEP

COMPOSED BY A. HOLZMANN

NEW YORK. C. H. DITSON & CO.

CHICAGO, ILL. LYON & HEALY.

TORONTO, CAN. WHALEY, ROYCE & CO.

PUBLISHED BY

FEIST AND FRANKENTHALER.

36 WEST 28th ST NEAR BROADWAY, NEW YORK

LONDON. B. FELDMAN 9 BERNERS STREET. W.

SAN FRANCISCO, CAL. SHERMAN, CLAY & CO.

CHICAGO, ILL. NATIONAL MUSIC CO.

A. H. GOETT ING. SPRINGFIELD. MASS.

SMOKY MOKES.

CAKE WALK and TWO STEP.

A. HOLZMANN.

TRIO.

38   "Smoky Mokes"

KERRY MILLS' TWO STEP MARCHES.
WHISTLING RUFUS
A CHARACTERISTIC MARCH
WHICH CAN BE USED EFFECTIVELY AS A
TWO-STEP, POLKA OR CAKE-WALK
BY
KERRY MILLS
COMPOSER OF
"RASTUS ON PARADE".
"HAPPY DAYS IN DIXIE."
"AT A GEORGIA CAMPMEETING."
ETC. ETC.
5
F.A. Mills
MUSIC PUBLISHER
NEW YORK
48 WEST 29th STREET.
CHICAGO.
CENTRAL MUSIC HALL BUILDG
COR STATE & RANDOLPH STS
SONG 5.

No cake walk given in the Black Belt District in Alabama was considered worth while attending unless "WHISTLING RUFUS" was engaged to furnish the music. Unlike other musicians RUFUS always performed alone, playing an accompaniment to his whistling on an old guitar, and it was with great pride that he called himself the "ONE-MAN BAND."

WHISTLING RUFUS.
A Characteristic Two Step March.

By KERRY MILLS.

Composer of { Rastus on Parade. Happy Days in Dixie. At A Georgia Campmeeting etc.

Trio.

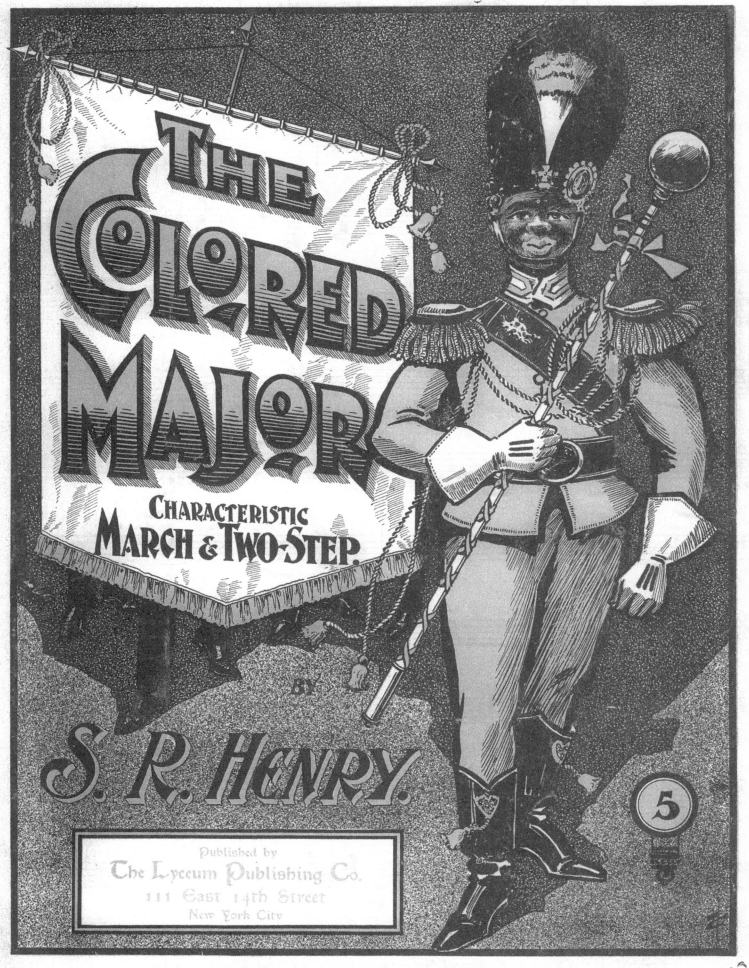

THE COLORED MAJOR.

CHARACTERISTIC MARCH AND TWO-STEP.

S.R.Henry.

Tempo di Marcia.

Jos. W. Stern & Co. Sole selling agents.

44

TRIO.

A Rag-Time March.

Creole Belles

Pub. for Band and Orchestra
**by H. N. WHITE
Cleveland, O.**

Band 50 cts.
Orchestra 10 pts 50 cts.
Orchestra 10 pts.& Piano 65 cts.
Full Orch. 80 cts.

5

By

J. Bodewalt Lampe.

PUBLISHED BY
THE LAMPE MUSIC Co
BUFFALO, N.Y.

Creole Belles.

RAG-TIME MARCH.

Band 50 cts.
Orchestra 10 pts 50 cts.
Orchestra 10 pts. & Piano 65 cts.
Full Orch. 80 cts.

J. BODEWALT LAMPE.

Spirito.

Lumb'rin' Luke.

Cake-Walk and Two-Step.

by. J. A. SILBERBERG.

Tempo di Marcia.

Piano.

TRIO.

54   "Lumb'rin' Luke"

Drum Solo.

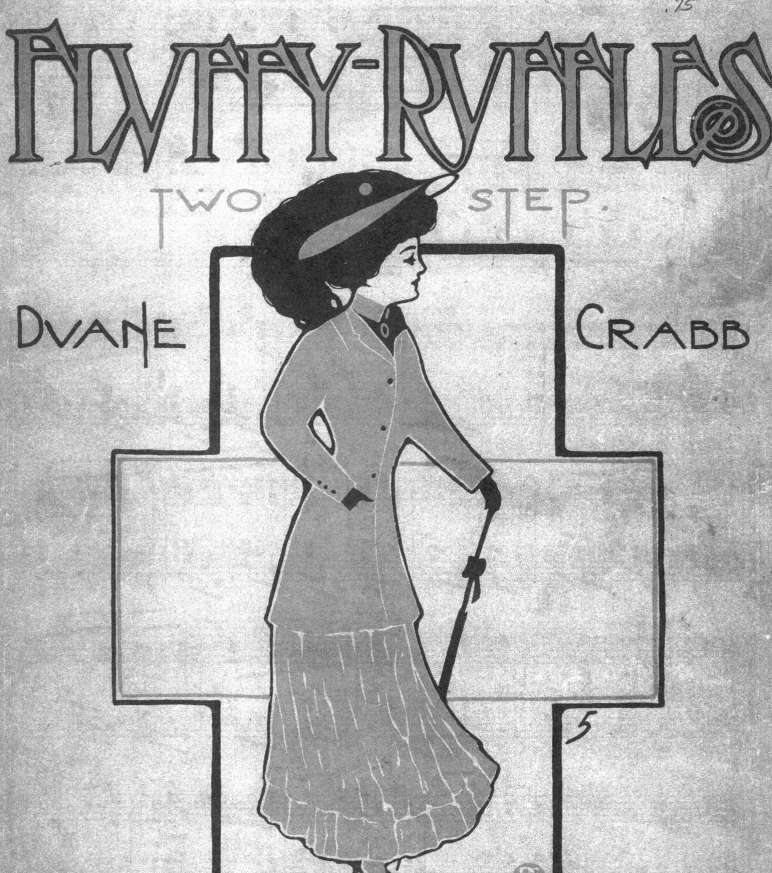

Fluffy Ruffles.

INTRO.
Moderato.

DUANE CRABB

57

ALL THE MONEY.

MARCH and TWO STEP.

RAYMOND BIRCH.

KERRY MILLS
RAG TIME DANCE

A CHARACTERISTIC
PIECE WHICH CAN
BE USED AS
ORCHESTRA

6

F. A. MILLS
122 WEST 36TH ST.
NEW YORK

Kerry Mills

"Kerry Mills Rag Time Dance."

By KERRY MILLS.

Tempo di Rago.

TRIO.

GRIZZLY BEAR
— Rag —

By GEORGE BOTSFORD

Moderato

TRIO.

PANAMA.
A Characteristic Novelty.

Wᵐ H. TYERS.
Composer of "La Trocha" "Maori" "Smyrna" etc.

TRIO.

Marcato il Melodie

THE CUBANOLA·GLIDE

R. G. ASHLEY

5

BY
HARRY·VON·TILZER
ALSO·PUBLISHED·AS·A·SONG

HARRY VON TILZER
MUSIC PUBLISHING CO.
125 W 43RD ST NEW YORK · MOREAU 1250 STRAND LONDON

GENE·BUCK

OUR·TRADE·MARK

The Cubanola Glide.

Slowly and Raggy.

by Harry Von Tilzer.

Trio.

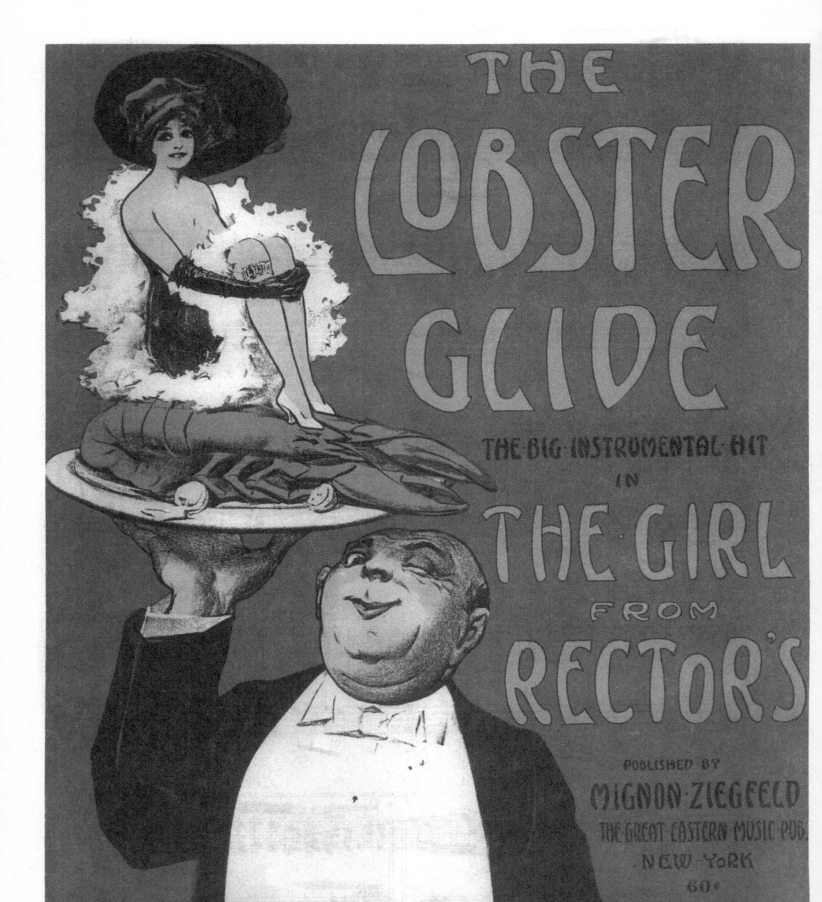

THE LOBSTER GLIDE.

MALVIN M. FRANKLIN.

TRÈS MOUTARDE
(Too much Mustard)
ONE OR TWO STEP

CECIL MACKLIN

Piano

Trio.

Donald Brian's Big Success in the Girl from Utah

Ballin' the Jack

Fox-Trot

BY CHRIS SMITH

ARRIA HATHAWAY AND JOE. McSHANE

101

Ballin' The Jack
Fox Trot

By CHRIS. SMITH
and
JAMES REESE EUROPE

BALLIN' THE JACK

CAROLINA FOX TROT

NEW SOCIETY DANCE

Originated by BILLY KENT & JEANETTE WARNER
AMERICA'S CLASSIEST DANCERS

by
WILL A VODERY

Published by JOS. W. STERN & CO.

50¢

Carolina Fox Trot.

NEW ONE-STEP.

WILL. H. VODERY.

(clap hands)

(clap hands.)

(Knock on Piano with knuckles.)

(Knuckles.)

THE REAL FOX TROT
THE CARUS BREEZE

COMPOSED BY
JACK GLOGAU

LEO FEIST NEW YORK

5

The Carus Breeze

FOX TROT

JACK GLOGAU

TRIO

THE CHEVY CHASE
FOX-TROT

by
J. Hubert Blake
(Eubie)

BETTY BOND

STARMER

50¢

Published by JOS. W. STERN & CO.

The Chevy Chase
Fox Trot

J. HUBERT BLAKE
(EUBIE)

"The Chevy Chase"

CRUEL PAPA!

FOX-TROT

BY WILL MARION COOK

Published by JOS. W. STERN & CO. 102-104 W. 38th St. NEW YORK CHICAGO and LONDON

LONDON JOS. W. STERN & CO.
ALBERT J. SON SIDNEY, AUSTRALIAN AGENTS

50

Cruel Papa!

Fox Trot

By WILL MARION COOK

DOCTOR BROWN

FOX TROT

by
FRED
IRVIN

5

JEROME H. REMICK & CO.

NEW YORK DETROIT.

DOCTOR BROWN
FOX TROT

by FRED IRVIN

"Doctor Brown"

Fizz Water
Trot and One Step

J. HUBERT BLAKE
(EUBIE)

Moderato

TRIO

124   "Fizz Water"

PALM BEACH

FOX-TROT

by

C. Luckyth Roberts

50¢

Published by Jos. W. Stern & Co.

Palm Beach

Fox Trot

C. LUCKYTH ROBERTS

Moderato

Trouville Canter.
Fox Trot.

H. WOODFORD.
Arr. by Will H. Vodery.

Moderato.
Slow with rythm.

131

Trio.

THE CASTLE

DOGGY-FOX-TROT

116142 PIANO SOLO 60¢

116143 10-CELLO & PIANO 50¢ NET

BY JAMES REESE EUROPE

G. Ricordi & C.

MUSIC · NEW YORK · PUBLISHERS

MILAN · ROME · NAPLES · PALERMO

LONDON · PARIS · LEIPSIG · BUENOS-AYRES

THE CASTLE DOGGY

Fox Trot

FORD T. DABNEY

JAMES REESE EUROPE

arr. by J. Louis von der Mehden, Jr.

"The Castle Doggy"

KANGAROO HOP

FOX TROT

MELVILLE MORRIS

PIANO

140

RABBIT'S FOOT

By
GEORGE L. COBB.

Rabbit's Foot

FOX TROT

GEORGE L. COBB

146   "Rabbit's Foot"

SHY AND SLY

TROT

BY

C. LUCKEYTH ROBERTS

116158 - Piano Solo - 60¢
116165 - 10 Cello & Piano - 50¢ net

G. Ricordi & C.
MUSIC · NEW YORK · PUBLISHERS
MILAN · ROME · NAPLES · PALERMO
LONDON · PARIS · LEIPSIG · BUENOS-AYRES

Shy and Sly
FOX TROT

C. LUCKEYTH ROBERTS.
Arranged by J. Louis von der Mehden, Jr.

TRIO

"Shy and Sly"